Past, Present or Future?

Decide whether the sentences are written in th
and match each one to the correct picture.

The wind blows loudly.

I cooked a big meal. •   •past

They will sing a happy song. •

He swims in the lake. •   •present

We will run in the park. •

My cat jumped up the steps. •

We walked in the forest. •   •future

Alphabetical Order

Sort the words into alphabetical order.

1. would   could   should

   _____ _____ _____

2. sink   pink   drink   think

   _____ _____ _____ _____

3. talk   walk   stalk   chalk

   _____ _____ _____ _____

4. round   sound   hound   mound

   _____ _____ _____ _____

5. night   might   light   fight

   _____ _____ _____ _____

Using a Dictionary

Use a dictionary to find the words. Circle the correct spellings.

fox
focks

coyn
coin

mowth
mouth

tadpole
tadpoal

trungk
trunk

nuespaper
newspaper

Write four of your favourite names in alphabetical order.

_____ _____ _____ _____

Plurals

Write the plurals on the lines and draw a picture to illustrate each one.

cross _____

drink _____

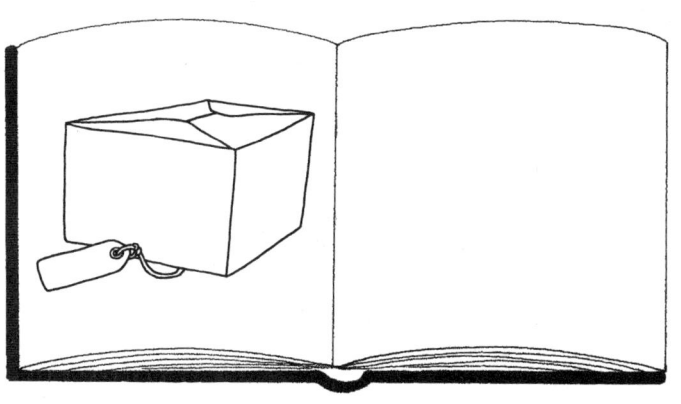
box _____

flower _____

woodpecker _____

sandwich _____

Action: Roll your hands over each other, like a mixer, and say ererer.

Read the words and draw a picture for each one.

river
summer
number
ladder
letter

Decorate the gingerbread friends. Do they have names?

Draw a house for the gingerbread friends to live in.

Using a Dictionary

Use a dictionary to find the correct spelling of each word and write them below the pictures.

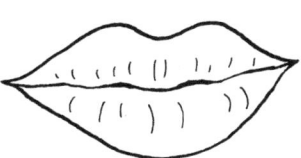
mowth

hors

beenstork

seagul

bicke

snoaball

stingk

burgur

tracter

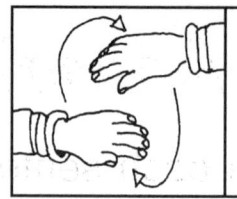

Action: Roll your hands over each other, like a mixer, and say *erererer*.

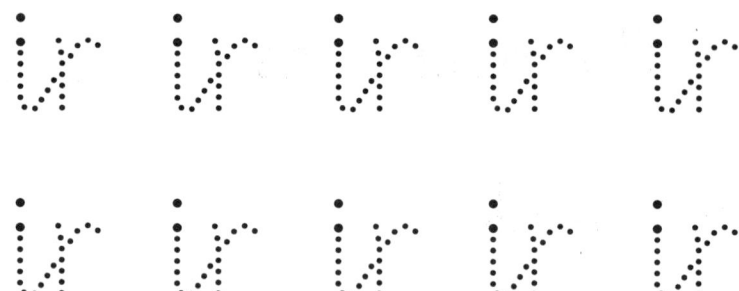

Look at the pictures and write a word for each one.

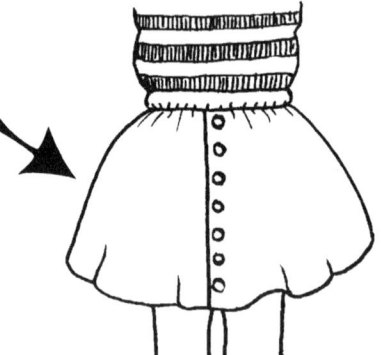

_____   _____   _____

_____   _____   _____

Adverbs

Add an **adverb** to complete each sentence. Use a dictionary if you do not know how to spell a word.

1. The river runs_____.

2. I drink_____.

3. The girl twirls_____.

4. He wept_____.

5. Zack thinks_____.

6. Snake hid_____.

7. I smiled _____.

8. Bee helped _____.

slowly
carefully
quickly
softly
noisily
sadly
happily
loudly
busily

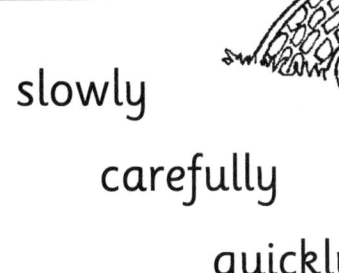
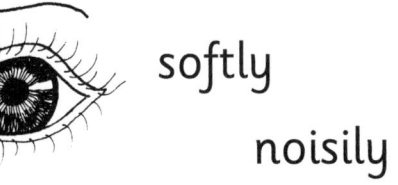

Action: Bang one fist on top of the other.

Word Webs

What words could you use instead of 'big'? Think of as many as you can and write them in the spaces of the word web.

Write the Words

Remember to use a dictionary if you do not know how to spell a word.

  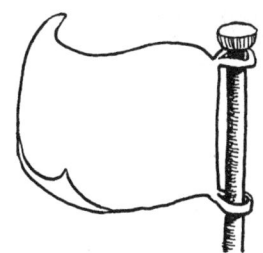

_____   _____   _____

  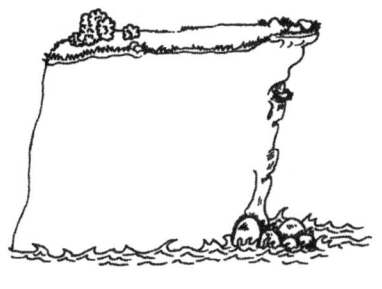

_____   _____   _____

_____   _____   _____

  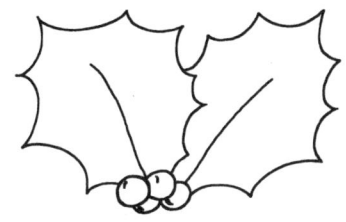

_____   _____   _____

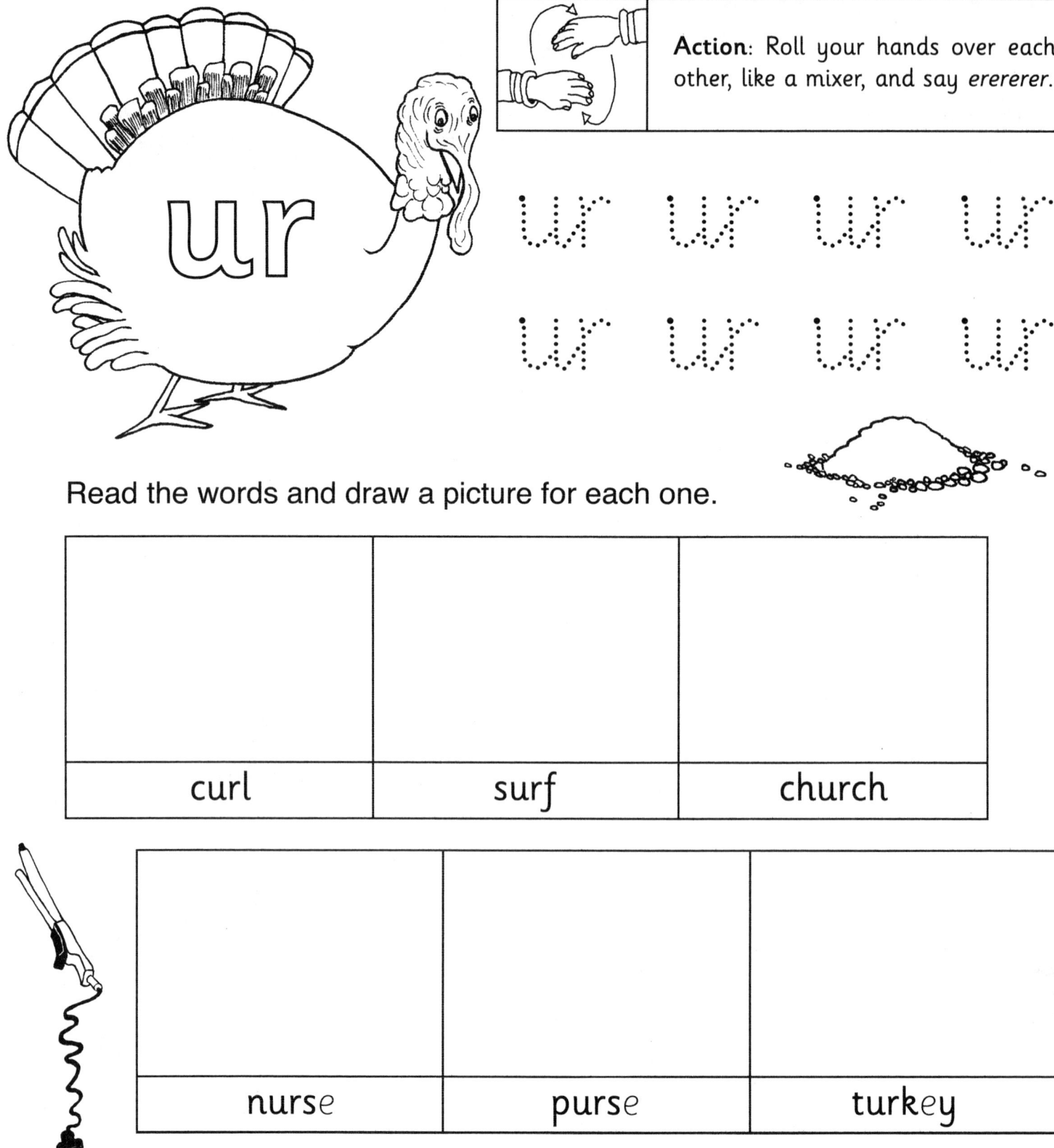

Antonyms

Write the opposite of each word and illustrate the words in the mirrors.

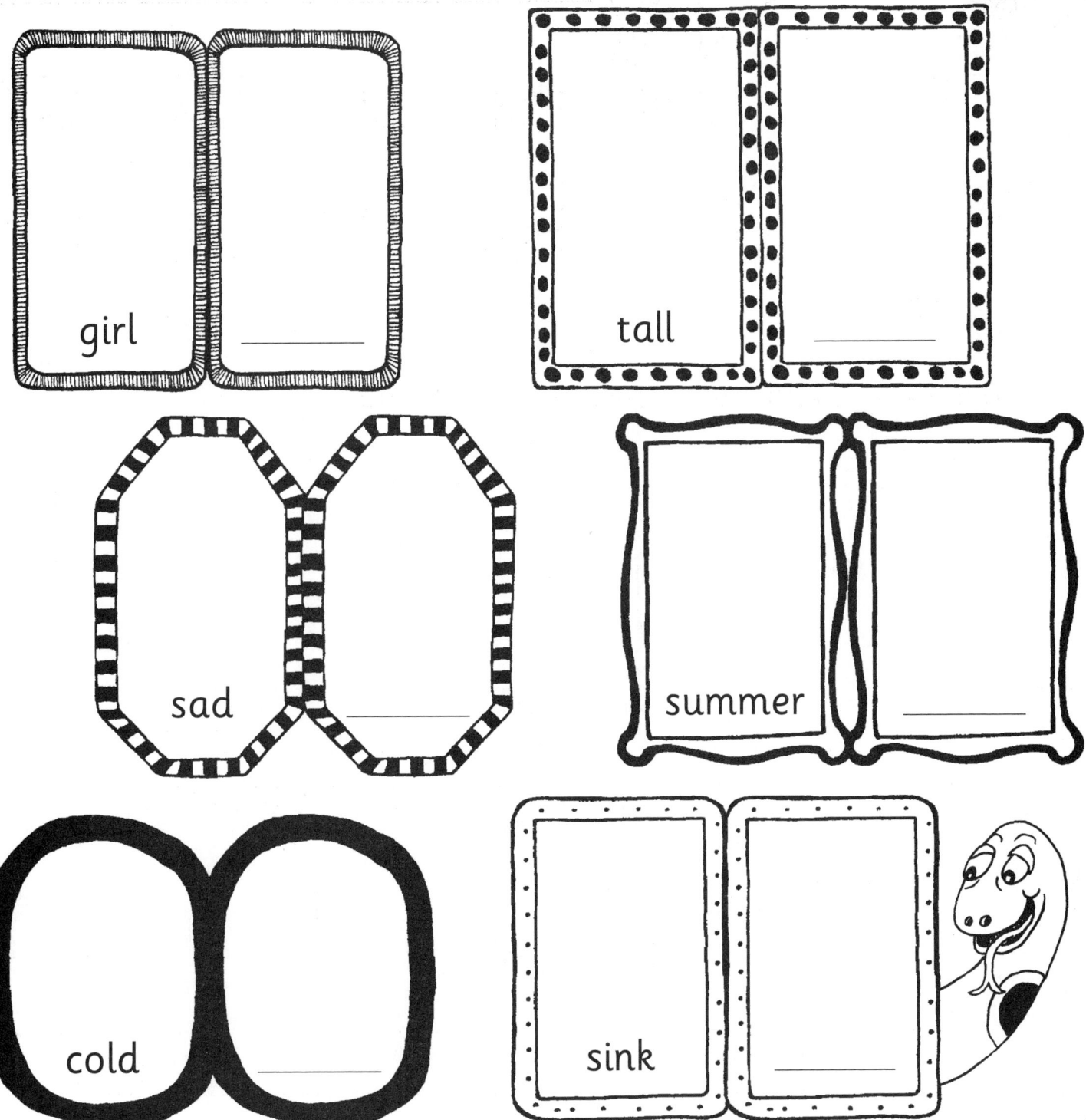

Questions

Decorate the question mark using your favourite colours.

why?

who?

which?

where?

what?

when?

Complete the questions by matching each question word to its correct ending.

What • • are you late?

Why • • way should we go?

Where • • is the time?

When • • is hungry?

Who • • are we leaving?

Which • • is my hat?

Action: Put your hands on your head, like a donkey pointing its ears down, and say *or*.

Draw a picture for each season.

spring | summer
autumn | winter

Word Webs

For each word think of another that has a similar meaning.

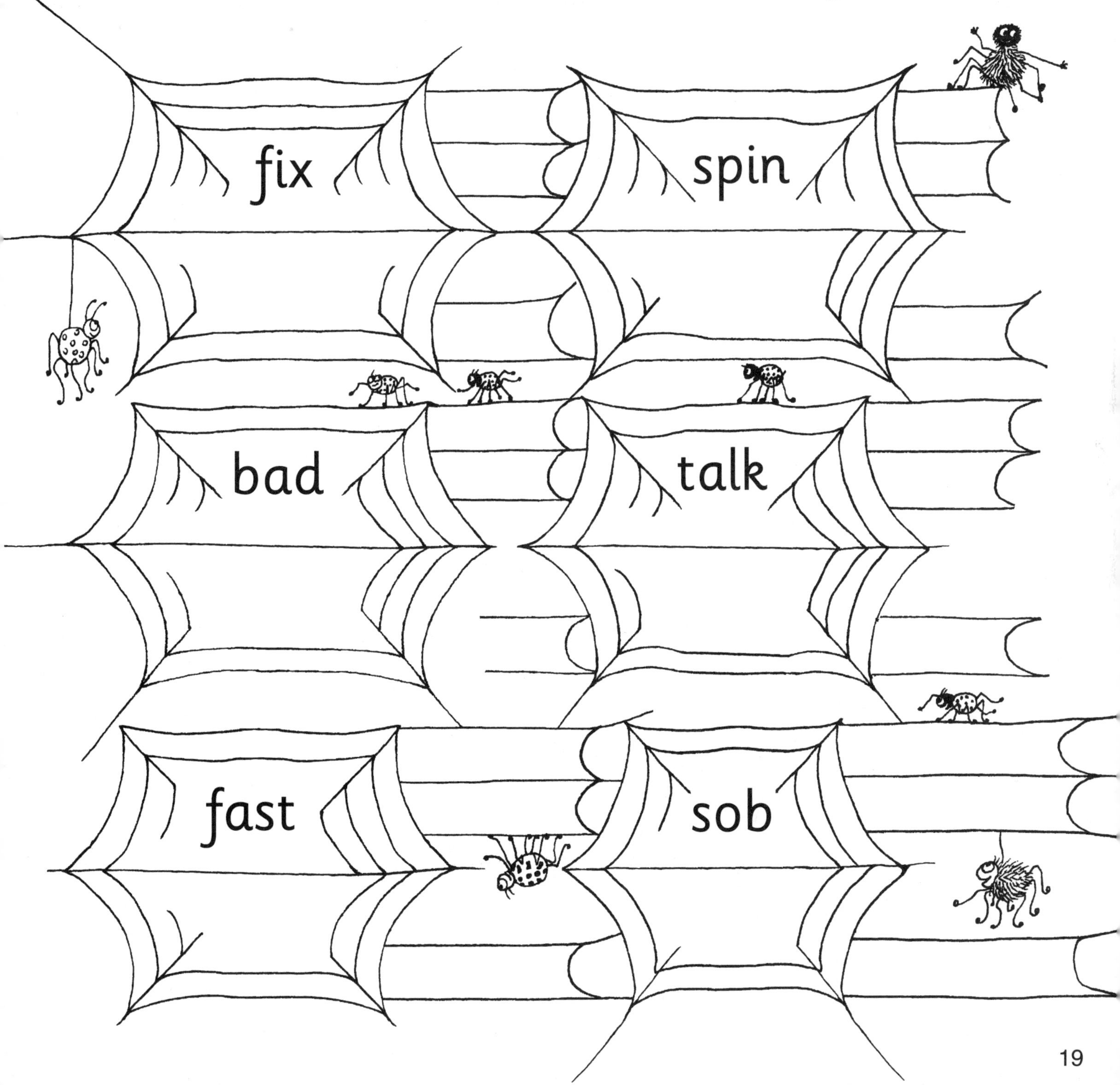

fix

spin

bad

talk

fast

sob

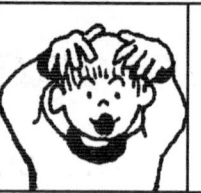

Action: Put your hands on your head, like a donkey pointing its ears down, and say *or*.

aw aw aw

aw aw aw

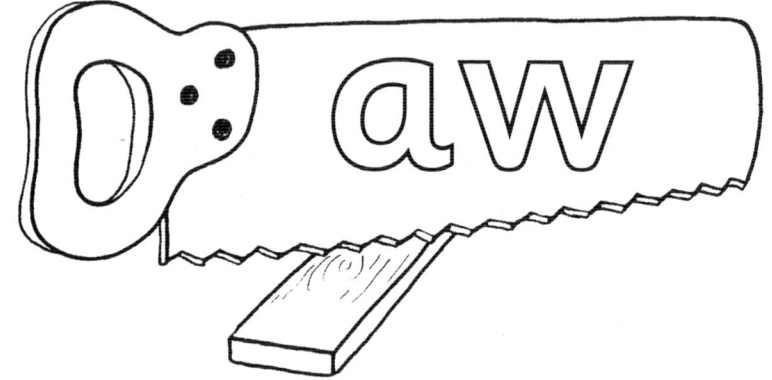

Read the words and draw a picture for each one.

paw hawk dawn

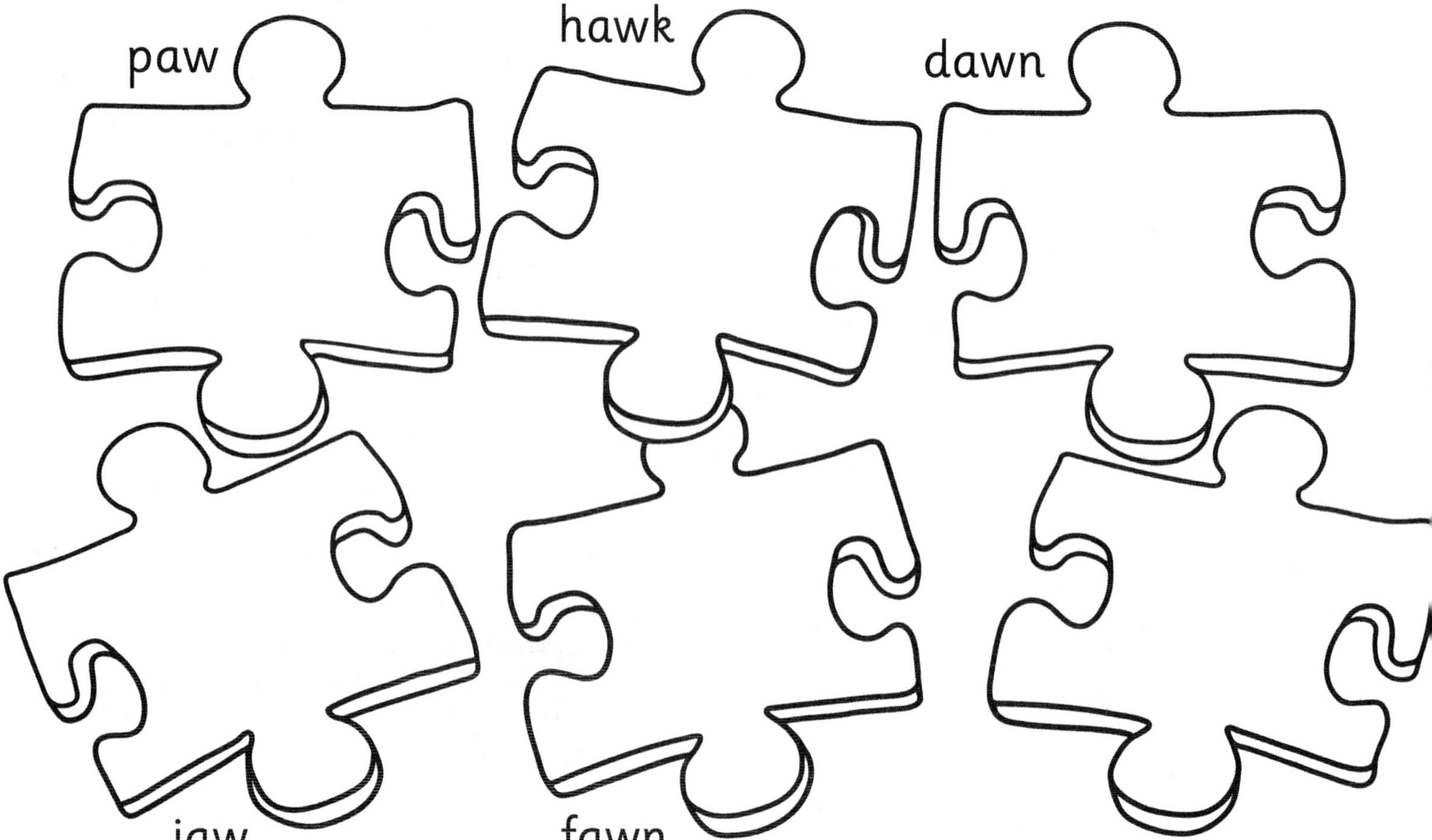

jaw fawn strawberry

Final Consonant Blends

Match each picture to the correct word and final blend.

21

Parts of Speech

Write two examples of each part of speech.

Common nouns ✏️ Black

_____
_____

Verbs ✏️ Red

_____
_____

Proper nouns ✏️ Black

_____
_____

 Adverbs ✏️ Orange

_____
_____

Pronouns ✏️ Pink

_____
_____

Adjectives ✏️ Blue

_____
_____

Parsing

Underline the different parts of speech using the correct colours. Look at the opposite page for a reminder of the colours.

1. Three ducks glide on the pond.

2. Aneeta picked a purple skirt and white shirt.

3. The big band played tunefully.

4. The brown horse galloped quickly.

5. They drank thirstily.

6. The small spider carefully spins a big web.

Tricky Words

Write over the dotted words. Then write them again on the line underneath.

once

upon

always

also

of

eight

love

cover

after

every

mother

father